WITH PAPER FOR FEET
Jennifer A. McGowan

ARACHNE PRESS

First published in UK 2016 by Arachne Press Limited
100 Grierson Road, London SE23 1NX

www.arachnepress.com

© Jennifer A. McGowan 2017

ISBN: 978-1-909208-35-3

The moral rights of the author have been asserted.

Printed on wood-free paper in the UK by TJ International, Padstow.

Supported using public funding by the National Lottery through Arts Council England.

SECTION FOUR

SECTION FIVE

WITH PAPER FOR FEET
SECTION ONE

WHITE WOMAN WALKS ACROSS CHINA WITH PAPER FOR FEET

Each night, the same approach to a different small house:
Qǐng nǐ, yī diǎn diǎn fàn, diǎn diǎn shuǐ. Wù yào chī fàn.
Please, a little rice, a little water. I need to eat. Duō xiè.
Thank you. The right words coming out of my *wài guó rén*
mouth.

Each night, setting up a bivvy against the wind, lighting
a small light, writing in my journal stories, memories,
forgotten names.

Sometimes I'd get lost in words, stay two or three days.
Children would approach: Nǐ weìshěnme gǎo cǐ a? *Why do
you do this?*

I'd reply Wǒ de mǔ qīn chūmò wǒ, *My mother haunts me,*
and they'd nod.

The brave would act out my need for a shrine. Sometimes
where I camped, I'd leave paper ribbons, small piles of stone.
Paper was the only thing to get heavier, not lighter, with use.
My words, my attempt to find my mother's birthscape, how
or if I could fit into it: heavy.

Yet for all my vocabulary I could not talk, could not trade
words, despite having paper for feet.

Could not send my words home, for I didn't know where, and what parcel box could fit all of me? Nine months of wandering, soaking my feet in flooded fields, pressing pulp to new paper, bleeding ink. White woman alone, her Chinese half never showing.

Finally at the foot of an anonymous hill my mother drifted in with the mist. Qǐng nǐ, māmā, gěi wǒ yī diǎn diǎn fàn. *Please, mother, give me something to live on.* I could not see her face, but before she dissolved she spoke my name.

THE TALKING SKULL
adapted from a Nigerian folktale

A hunter
in search of food for his family
walked and walked
but found no prey.
The plains stretched on
and the sun beat
and he was weary.

There was one tree
that stretched its branches
and he sat beneath it.
Propped his feet
on a white rock
and drank.
When he was rested, he noticed
the rock had two eye-holes
and teeth. Alone
in the vast expanse
except for the sky,
he addressed the rock
in a casual fashion:
'What brought you here, my friend?'
Then he laughed,
grateful no one could hear him.

So perhaps it is to be forgiven
if the hunter jumped
when the skull fixed him
in its empty gaze and said,
'Talking brought me here!'

Food and family forgotten,
the hunter ran to the king
to tell him of this wonder
and the king
and all his attendants
went in stately fashion
to see the talking skull.

The plains stretched on
and the sun beat
so it is perhaps to be forgiven
if the king was weary
and rather hot and bothered
when at last they reached the one tree
that stretched its branches.

The king ordered the hunter
to show him the wonder
and the hunter found the skull
and addressed it in a friendly fashion:
'Greetings again! Please tell my king–
what brought you here?'

But the skull
was silent.

For a long time
the hunter pleaded and implored
questioned and queried
but the skull
might well have been
a white rock to prop his feet on
for all the good it did.

The king was angry.
He had come a long way
and had expected wisdom from beyond the grave
or at least a miracle
that befit his station.
He had his champion
lop off the hunter's head
and began the long trip home.

Beyond the one tree
the plains stretched on.
Beneath the tree
the skull rolled grinning
over to the hunter's head and asked,
'What brought you here, my friend?'
And the hunter's head said sadly,
'Talking brought me here!'
And underneath the shaded earth
other skulls set up a clattering.

THE WITCH-BOX

Hide the skin of a seal-woman. She'll cry
of course, but she'll marry you.

Teach her the rhythms of your day. Breakfast.
Commuting. Nightly pleasures. Teach her

to worship the sun rather than weep
at the moon's pull. Your children will be strong,

go into a trade where there's water. Mind
you keep some things to yourself:

shake three grains of salt from the witch-box
every night into each corner of the house;

make sure, last thing last, the skin is locked up
tighter than a shotgun. Mind, now.

If she finds it—if she slips into her unforgotten self—you'll find
yourself ebbing; you'll shatter the witch-box, drink only salt
wine.

PHANTOM PAINS

It happened the week after I chopped down the hawthorn.
A knife-slip, a welter of blood, and time shifts.

Woollen clothes, straw prickling my skin, I moan
in a smoky half-light. A beldame crouches at my feet,
encouraging me to breathe. (This is the time
I die in childbirth. My husband is a woodcutter.)

A hundred years later, my brother is taken by fairies.
Mother and Father talk in whispers through the night,
and Mother cries. My best enemy, Jennet Clark,
tells me he's run off to sea, or to London–the story
changes with each telling; the important thing is
he doesn't want us, and that it hurts–but Father
hangs horseshoes, and buries a witch-bottle
under the threshold for good measure.
            When the next baby is a girl,
and she deformed, even Jennet is silenced. Father
cuts down a stand of thorn in revenge. I go to town
to be prenticed, and the house burns. I am shunned
as bad luck.

            Later still, I take to dancing
in fairy rings, bedecked with ribbons and the witching smile
of youth. Lovers and swains–I leave no hayrick
undisturbed, no bed of moss untried. The man I marry
is understanding, perhaps more than I deserve, and we wed
in May, with blossom everywhere, before I start to show.
The child is healthy, but I suffer the wages of sin.

(That time, it's plague.) Hardly any rest
before the world spins and I remember Paris
in all its tumult, its shame and glory. We cheer Madame
in the square and plant thorn on the graves to keep
the bastards quiet.

        Britannia rules the waves.
A Navy wife, I wax and wane with the fortunes
of the sea. Guilty, he throws trinkets over his shoulder to
appease: gewgaws, curios, fetishes, anything
ornate that takes his interest.
I don't know what half the carvings are, but I suspect,
especially when a visiting professor coughs and refuses to
take tea in the front room.
        Superstition spreads like wildfire. My husband
turns merchant, transfers to India. I go with. Cholera.

Now there is the hum of white lights and pungent antiseptic.
Voices murmur, then chitter, and I open my eyes.
My neighbour found me on the floor, summoned, she says,
by an 'unearthly shriek.' I'm in a thick fug of morphine.
My words come out mutterings, imprecations, poetry.

No one knows plants like I do. Sometimes a ball flies
into the marjoram, and the kids dare each other to fetch it.
Before they do, I come to the gate. They shuffle. I could
offer: flowers, pearls, cookies,
        but they want only one thing.
I point down the road with the fingers I no longer have,
shout, and hurl the ball past them like a curse.
Delighted, they scatter. A cat weaves around my legs,
cementing the effect. I go in. I make tea. Night comes.

MARA SPEAKS

You come down from the north,
bodies restless and disjoint,
aging, some cottoned in darkness
which will lift, but barely.
Look, you say, look what we have done.
Jubilation and death both.
I can read them in your scars,
the raw pulsing at the edge of vision
where losses remain. Not even
my hands can heal them, these spaces
where gods and lovers have lived.

You need something to fill your eyes,
to hide you from yourselves, each other, sleep.
Tell us about your son, you say,
and I realise this is it,
the moment when I am no longer who I am,
but what I carry, have carried,
child of desire, night's dreaming, as far beyond my knowing
as my need is beyond yours.
No mother keeps her child forever,
I know, but I thought the lasting would be longer,
the parting more than a sharpened demand.
Men of blood and men of binding,
witch-women and women of steel
for whom the body is no more than
gobbets of flesh, a god a sacrifice, crying:
Tell us, show us, give us
not the pain, that's not interesting,
not the secrets you learned to keep you alive,
but the shining, the one, bright-burning, the answer,

we need a guide and a reason to gore our blades
and he'll do just fine.

I weigh what I give you, who know how to take,
who have no children and keep no gods.
Mother, priestess, prophetess, I speak
(I'm skilled enough at speaking sideways)
but the words are mine, mark them,
they bite. And if I give of myself
it is for my sake alone;
and not because of you, or your hunger,
or your fears, or your pains,
but for love of a west-eyed woman
who knows the worth of a night's dreaming
and who knows, like me, the meaning of hope.

SOMETHING ABOUT LOVE

She had the smallest waist,
so how the queen could lace her tighter
taught us a lot about hate.
My brother dwarves unlaced her,
but not before my breath also stopped.

She had the cleanest hair,
and it shone–a hundred brush-strokes
every night. When the queen
gave her the poisoned comb,
it told us a lot about envy.
My brothers washed her in wine
and she gasped, but not before
my limbs also grew heavy.

She had the sweetest breath,
so we didn't know about the apple
till the prince persuaded us
he knew more about love,
and we let her go.

At Christmas now,
an owl brings me bright ribbons.
A raven, a lock of hair.
A dove, sweet fruits.
I chase dust-bunnies. My brothers
work to craft her children toys.

Because of what we learned
there is no bitterness.
Because of what we saw
there is no sorrow.
We are simple men,
but we do know something
about love.

SONG OF KRAMPUS

All year I gather birch twigs,
gather them up into bundles, just so.
Tie them carefully. Make sure
the heft is right for shins
and backsides. At the end of November
I begin blackening: rubbing coal dust and ash
into my already-dark hide until
I leave smoky footprints.

Oh, child, when you feel my stings
will you realise at last I'm the only one
to care about the naughty?
The chuckling saint only brings gifts
for those sweeter than spun sugar.
Too much sweetness attracts flies, like dung.

Let us dance. You hide behind the chair.
I snarl and flash my sharpened teeth.
Around and around each piece of furniture
until you tire and my switches
tease your skin. Your parents will hang
my golden bundle–my gift–for you
to look at year-long, while your spun-silk
sister's doll will break in a week, maybe two.

Listen at the window for my chain-call.
Don't reach for spun sugar. It shatters.

LOVE LIKE SALT

A pearl sweats near poison.
A king holds a jewelled cup,
seated between the daughter who chose gold
and the one who would go bare for no man,
but the poison at the feast is subtle:
an empty chair and ancient guilt.

A servant brings the cook
to account for the tasteless meat.
The king almost sees,
but does not hesitate to blame.
The girl does not quail;
says, 'Once you cast forth a child
because you thought she loved you less.'
He lowers his head, weeps.

She embraces him at last,
whispering his name,
knowing
she has made him
eat his words
and knowing nothing else
to rub in.

THE HOOD

Red, spread, tread, fed, shred, dead.
Step by step, that's how it went.

I covered her, muffled her perceptions.
A meal for one on the way to Granny's.

The prettiest flower blooms once a lifetime.
She left the path. I exposed a shoulder:

a feast for hungry eyes.
　　　　　A bass, needy demand:
she gives way, steps in. Caught on the threshold,

I begin to unravel. Then cast off, like prudence;
molted, like fur. Long arms rip and tear.

Rags, I soak up the stains.

IN GRANNY'S HOUSE

Six weeks in bed,
and the stink of piss.
No one to cook–to light a fire–
let alone empty the pot.
Just curl up under the quilt, woman.
Don't sob. Wait.

The door is on the latch.

My husband insisted we live here,
then got felled by a tree.
And I, stuck here, lost–
my daughter seduced into town.
Never coming. She hates the forest,
fears the dark. So do I.

The door is on the latch.

The hunger eats me.
I wait for the one
I knitted my fingers for,
her smile opium-bright.
For her–or for someone
to free me.

The door is on the latch.

MR. FOX

Be bold.
She goes through the gateway
to the house in the woods,
knowing, by her blood's pounding,
that truth lives here,
and not in the townhouse
where she met him.
Through the front door
(unlocked) and up the stairs,
where the wide, untidy bedroom
still smells of him.
She tries to piece together
the real story, the one
he never told her, the one
she deduced from
a hair on his shirt,
a stray glance. Downstairs next,
to the stained door
which sticks and smells damply
of rust. Needing to know,
she forces it, stumbles, finds herself
treading on skeletons and charnel.

A noise–an echoing laugh
or scream.
Be not too bold:
she hides.
Dragging her could-be twin,
he enters, chops her double down,
mislays a hand, leaves.

At the denouement,
the great engagement feast,
her brothers tear him to shreds
like hounds. She creeps upstairs,
hides her locket
in a bureau drawer;
returns over the months for a look,
searching for the sign she missed,
never sure whether his sharp-toothed grin
showed him the master of caprice
or candour.

BIRD VERDELIÒ

*O Bird Verdeliò, o bird Verdeliò, make me more beautiful than I
am–Cenerentola before the ball*

It's strange the way things go.
My Cenerentola–well, I didn't know
what I was in for when I let
her father take me home.
It was a migrating instinct,
a wish to nest in summer.

She said my name;
my sun shone. Ash could not disguise
the music of her speech.
And so beguiled, I would
make her more beautiful
or more ugly than she was
so she could feather her own nest
with dreams.
        When I could see
        that cinders no longer
        would weigh her down or protect her,
I extracted this promise: to be near her always.
So I gave her again the dress of the colours of heaven
and she limped one-shoed to her story's end.

But it wasn't the end. Every day
she feeds me with her shining hand
and my song becomes more beautiful than it was.
She is all the colours of heaven;
I sing and sing and sing.

BRIAR ROSES

On Christmas Day the skeletons of the boys who failed
hang on the briars like ornaments.
They rattle and almost hiss
as they retreat before the chosen one,
who might not be special
save for his crown and timing.

He kisses her. Eyelids flicker.
Briars melt. She smiles,
no longer perfect or immortal.

The marriage proceeds. The bride blushes
and begins to decay.
Bones decorate the lawns
like jewels.

CINDERELLA'S MOTHER

The amber light branches and streams
over the tree on the grave.
An ash-girl
becomes a princess again,
casts aside her years of duty
for a short night of chandeliers and dancing.

When Ella marries
and moves to the palace
the tree settles into being itself.
No more teenaged demands.
No more salty rain.
A little jenny wren builds a nest
and brings up her broods,
never favouring one child
above another.

THE MAIDEN WITHOUT HANDS
For A. Sexton, angrily

No woman can speak
without hands.

Once
the Devil fell in love
with a pretty girl, tricked her father,
and came to carry her off.
So she tricked herself out
in her finest, drew a chalk circle,
and he could not enter.
I'll come back on Friday, said the Devil.
Make sure she doesn't wash.

Next she took refuge in salt.
Her hands were washed clean.
Off they came: Forgive me, daughter,
and of course she did, because she was good.
But her stumps were two salt circles
that the Devil couldn't pass;
so she traded in her home and the Devil as well,
one father for each hand,
and set off. She was tidy;
had her arms bound behind her
so their flapping wouldn't offend.

For a while she was free.
She bothered nobody, nobody spoke to her.
But who could replace what she'd lost?
Who knew of her hunger?
I know, she thought,

and got herself another father–he'd know what to do.
At least this one was clean.
Dear God, she said. I believe your word.
That was the last she said.
And miracles happened.
Food, husband, and all.
Silver hands no one could touch,
specially fashioned by her husband
whom she couldn't touch, either.
But he could touch her, and left her
well on the way to motherhood,
making him the fourth father.
Take care of her, he said.

When his son (of course) was born,
his mother sent word, since the girl
couldn't tell him herself.
But the Devil played the stronger hand,
and rewrote the letter. You know the rest.
He changed the next three as well,
and the girl and the child
were thrown into the wilderness,
out of pity. She took refuge in tears,
and sure enough
since she was clean and tidy,
baby and arms bound up behind her,
her Father looked after her
and her hands grew back,
so when her husband found her
they lived happily, and only for each other.

So they say.
She was always the Silver-Handed Queen.
Not the flesh, but the silver were always on show
and the king loved to tell the story
of how God and love conquered the Devil
and how if you're good and patient and tidy
with your arms tied behind you
things will all come right in the end, won't they my dear.
A nod followed, and usually a smile.

Maybe you're wrong, good Mother,
good brothers. Maybe they're not real hands.
After all, she never says a thing.
It's her fathers' bargain: a nod, a smile,
while you write the story with a stronger hand.

THE HORSES OF THE SEA
after W.B. Yeats

Visionary-mad, he faces down the host,
cries defiance at their battle-cars.
Bare-chested, the warrior wades waist-deep,
fighting against the tidal flow of blood.
For want of sense, he swings his sword
against imagined enemies. To realise
the red salt on his hands is son's blood
is death, yet death is all he knows.
While Emer weeps, Cu Chulainn fights
the horses of the sea. They buck and rear.
Though his arm is flesh and not the moon,
they fear its strength.

CURANDERO
after Pablo Amaringo

I sing
a circle. I sing you
into the circle, sing the vapours
out of you, bring you
before the one you have offended,
teach you to be clean. Look,
I touch your belly. Look,
I touch your head. The brown vapour
leaves you. The brown vapour
leaves you. The snakes
in your belly leave.
Listen. I sing you. The tall man,
the magician in the trees,
must not be mocked.
Here he is. Say your sorries.
Listen: I clean you. I teach you
to be clean. This is the song
the trees taught me.

ICARUS

In my mind's eye you are
suspended, handsome
but perilously young

and love is the second-best thing.

Some people plumb
any depth they can manufacture
but you looked up,
could not rest
until you reached beyond.
Poetry, drugs, mountain-climbing, sky-diving:
afterwards there was always *down*.

Till one redwood summer
we were small among giants
and the sun
streamed through
in dusty prayers

we had never touched
so much, walked
so far holding hands

your face suffused with the light.

Next morning
leaving only a few scattered pills
you left

eyes turned upwards
hand stretched
toward the trees
you flew beyond

A SORT OF LOVE STORY

If I were a were-elephant,
in the night I would trumpet love loud and long,
till the elephant equivalent of high C
would make the moon explode
and I would sneeze gouts of flame
out my schnoz and sharpen my tusks
on your front door till that last barrier broke down
and you recognised me by the light of the burning moon
and you would take matters into your own hands
(because a fiery elephant is more than a handful)
and try to get bitten by a were-something-else
so that we could ride our lunatic fluxes together,
but it wouldn't be that simple: in your quest
to be bitten by a were-tarantula
you would cut your hand on a banana display and become
a were-fruitstand, and whilst you would sate
my full appetite for bananas (is that elephants or monkeys?)
it would hardly be the basis for a fulfilling bipartisan
relationship, now, would it?
                              So put aside the tendency
to believe we can only be satisfied by the improbable.
Take my hand, touch my cheek, and we will make love
by the light of a reasonable moon.

WITH PAPER FOR FEET
SECTION TWO

SONG OF THE ARMS OF A MAN
after E.F. Taylor

I sing in the arms of a man.
We who, separated by fate,
by a much-regretted golden band
taken on at nineteen, are exiles,
buffeted on sea and land by violence
of passion, chased by unremitting wrath,
can find no realm nor any destined shore
to rest upon–help me, o muse, tell
of the strength of his embrace,
of goodness so wondrous stars know of it.
How broiled his life in endless cares,
yet he traverses perils to come to me,
endlessly waiting. What is the cause
we are so hated by rosy-fingered dawn,
by lawyers saying there is no release?
Are the heavens so hemmed about
in high resentment? Let me kneel,
here, where our bed is still warm,
pray we endure and will at long last lie
unhaunted on the shores of our desire.

HELEN: MENELAUS, ETC.

With him I was the queen of sheep and dung.
With Paris, magic and love. Talk about a no-brainer.
Those years in his trophy room, on a shelf
like a golden apple but dusted less, got to me.
He aspired to godhead, just not mine.
It wasn't the sex I disliked, it was the lack of contact.
Oh, he'd praise my swansoft hair, decorate it
with gems, as long as it gleamed like gold.
I fancied being a redhead once. He threw fits.
Insisted I dress like a statue. What a man.
Didn't know what he'd had till he lost:
I rode astride out the gate with my wide-eyed boy.
Troy wasn't a new chapter; it was a new book.
A blank one I could actually write in.
Hecuba wanted more daughters. We got on.
Andromache knew how to whistle. Et ceterae.
So good to be in the company of women!
Equals, I mean, not averted-eye slaves
trained to service their masters on the QT.
I had my choice of outfits. P. loved them all,
the simpler the better. I dressed once as a shepherdess–
he actually cried.
                    I forgot the agreement.
All my ex-suitors marched as one.
I had my spies (see aforementioned slaves).
It wasn't loyalty or their 'sacred word'.
They hoped he'd die in battle. That's all.
Then they'd rumble for me. Holy fuck.
I despised them all. I'd lie by the Scamander,
disguised as a beggar, charcoal, soap-flakes in my hair,
and dream the death of Sparta. They never knew.

I could teach Achilles a thing or two.
Ten too-short years of passion, till the gods
(and Odysseus) got bored. Never invite family.
Then death, yes, mourning, dreams dragged through the dust.
You never know how a broken heart sears
till you're related to the sun. I burned to ash.
Everything else burned thereafter. I forgot how to cry.
Lacedaimonian shouts out my window: I made sure to bathe.
I waited there, shining, in my nest of light,
the gleaming one, pretty girl, spoils of war.
Then home again, to live out my shelf-life.
Should have listened to Mother. She knew
women don't get happy endings. We bear and are borne away.

So there were worse things than death, though
I had to wait till Faust for good sex.
And now, stuck here, in dull echoes of history,
I compose myself. Write this down:
'Here lies Helen, beloved of Troy, who never
gave a damn about Sparta, and vice versa.'
The war was just and only his pride.
Got that? Listen and learn. Go make movies.
Tell jokes if you must. Just don't tell more lies.
And stay away from the bloody swans.

TROY: SEVEN VOICES

I. PATROCLUS

Gold is heavy,
and chafes.

Still
the fear of who I'm not
is effective,
the desperate pause
as I approach
making the thrust easy, and then
the soft sibilance
of blood on the ground.

Who'd have thought
one dice game
and a teenage crush
would lead to these endless forays
against the walls,
this skilled impersonation?

I've done more than fifty, I bet.
My arm is almost tired.
I stretch as Chiron taught us
crack my neck
and stride forward.

At last.
Hector.

II. GREEK SOLDIER

All we wanted
was to get a glimpse of her.
The one we'd come for. The one
made fools of kings
and warriors of farmers.

Each morning
before dawn
before the light could betray us
we'd scan the walls
and the tower windows
for a sight.

We never got one.
Throughout the years of fighting,
these years of boy into man
we dreamed. Silently
to each other we'd relate
our stories of her, the way she'd look sideways
and knees that never knew fear
would buckle. How her eyes
shone like lightning
and burned.

And how at the end
the one we'd all come to
we'd hear quiet footsteps
and the white fingers that closed our eyes
would be soft as featherdown
and one bright tear
would be our swansong.

III. SCAMANDER

I have carried this weary leaf
from hoary mountain slopes over rocks
past thirsty roots and wading herons
past shoals of trout, silver-scaled,
to this broad plain. Now my waters swell
to flood. Armour and keepsakes sink.
I bring the detritus of flesh
with its seeping red
to the receiving sea
where all burdens are absorbed
and nameless.

IV. ASTYANAX

Just a moment of flight
was all there was.

V. POLYXENA

Dear Achilles,

I didn't want this.
Not the fame,
not the long blue gaze
over my brother's body
that drowned us.

When I threw my bracelets down
from the tower to make up
Hector's ransom, I was throwing you away,
knowing you'd not survive him long.

I should have known
a self-love big as yours
wouldn't rest in an easy grave.
Even dead you must get
what you want.

So I dress
as if for my wedding
while Andromache and my women
mourn. But let me tell you,
my blood
will bring you no peace.

When I fall
I will fall with the weight of Troy
and my shade's arms
around your neck
will be a millstone.

VI. CASSANDRA

Listen to me: looks aren't everything,
but they help. Sixteen and cursed by a god–
well, that wasn't good, but once the walls fell
and knives were everywhere, a tear-stained
and pretty face was my ticket back to life.
A trophy's not the best option, but as a princess,
let's face it, I was born to belong to someone,
whatever name you put on it.

I look at these new and proud owners
and see beyond them to their deaths.
Some by women's hand; some by fire;
others by neglect, as war wounds infect
and incapacitate. Agamemnon, now,
he goes home to a story
they'll be telling for years. He's forgotten
he married Helen's sister,
who comes with her own price
and a lifetime grudge of being second.

The shadows of Troy are long. What they touch
will falter. The gods must have tragedy.
Speaking of which, my vision clouds again:
I hear screams and tears
and the thunk of the axe.
It shouldn't come as a surprise
that I'm as mortal as you are,
but, like you, I don't listen.

VII. HECUBA

Ancient bitch, empty dugs–
battling for scraps, for
the smallest thing to crunch
between blunted teeth.

You'd think, wouldn't you,
that fifty sons would be enough.
That one would be left.
Instead, pyre after pyre,
when I even got that,
and a husband cut down at the altar.
An embarrassment of corpses.

Not that I was embarrassed.
They all fought well. We weren't the invaders.
Only Paris, smitten, young,
not old enough not to pray,
believed a promise. He always was a fool,
but he had the sweetest voice
and a smile would charm you
every time.

So fifty sons dead. Good as.
My daughters? I can't bear to think.
I should have listened to Cassandra,
looked that gift horse in the mouth,
something. Anything.

But the gods
in their slanted pity
changed me to run through the night
and whine.

And I did run. To the bowels of boats,
hiding in cargo, then on land
through forests, valleys, even backyards
if the night was thick enough.
I followed the Greeks' bloody footsteps
with my own raw ones.

On these black slopes now
under a hunter's moon
I stalk their children

and howl curses
to ever darker

and more ancient gods.

TROY: AFTER THE HORSE

The first real shock wave
hit when Hector fell, though panic
had been years in building.

Now fire is king. Citizens take
what is least flammable and flee.
Survivors learn to walk
through the ghosts of walls.
Wives and princesses go missing in back alleys.

So freed of all constraint
save the future, Aeneas takes
his father on his back.
The world's weight presses him on.

PYTHONESS

You never really get used to the taste
of laurel leaves, you know?
That hard green bitterness
which leads to ecstasy, divinity,
and a steady income.

The first time I sat on the tripod
suspended over the chthonic rift,
I said *You must be joking.*
Never so uncomfortable, and the cloying smell!
Now, said the elder,
you see why we rotate.

Years later, hair unbound
and eyes streaming–my first time in public.
In front of me, two bodies all scraped knees
and clasped hands, asking
How can we conceive? We all fall still,
listening for words.
I chew another wad. Eyes stare and hope.

And then I get it. You don't
put your ear to the ground for a sun god.
We're here to listen
for the roots Daphne sprouted
when she escaped, burrowing down to Persephone,
who understood. Their knowledge
cracks the earth, becoming steam
no male sky can carry.

This is our secret.

Another secret is that compassion can mingle with truth.
I look at the twining hands.
Words come.

TEMPUS FUGUE

It's never wise to make love to a god.
I say *love*, as if
they understand the concept,
or anything except *want* and how to take.
Only worship, however perfunctory or bleary-eyed,
freely willed or surrendered, like a body,
appeases. You may find yourself reborn:
tree, river, star, what have you.
I'd say it's a different sort of freedom,
this altered consciousness, this will
not to remember, if only
I could move. As it is
I'm stuck, a monument to desire.
Which isn't bad, the flesh-on-flesh,
those twining arms, feet curled round about,
that catch of breath, the final dying sigh–
if it's all you have. Most of us, however,
have mothers, brothers, lovers
it will be impossible to explain this to
after the last time. And so forth.
Gods alone exist in the vacuum
of self-definition. The rest of us
are defined by others' eyes and expectations.
Saying that, I'm almost sure I had hands,
hair down to my bum, green eyes,
the works. Now
I'm not what they see. They come to me
with prayers and offerings, as if my scars
were holy, as if to touch something
that has touched the divine offers immunity.
Well guess what. You can pray all you want.

Just don't expect an answer, or not
the one you were looking for. I don't
remember faces, but yours will get you in trouble,
I'm willing to bet. You're too fit, too ripe
for running. Which, incidentally, won't work. I tried.
Not that I don't envy you, with the wind in your hair.
I'd give it all, the alleged wisdom,
the blessings, all the blind prayers
to feel the sweet, aching warmth
of the earth beneath my toes again.
Instead of which
I have a half-life, half-death.
A sort of blank immortality;
part of a landscape without a face.

So I'll outlast you. So what?
I have nothing
to measure myself by. Unlike
when I was a girl/nymph/woman,
when words like 'season' had meaning.
When hours had weight. When life
had limits. When time
was the only answer there was.

WITH PAPER FOR FEET
SECTION THREE

EMILIA

So, speaking as I thought, I died.
And now, Iago, you can't shut me up.
All your secret peccadilloes discovered:
how you were rubbish in bed, cold and bossy
and dreaming of Moorish heat.
Yes, I knew. You and Desdemona
say the same things in your sleep.
Said, I should say. She's crossed over, too;
we sing and gossip together in the endless nights.
We're putting on a production of Aristophanes.
Lysistrata.
Desdemona and the Nurse (a refugee
from some other murders) made the masks.
And the phalluses. I tried, but have never seen anything decent
to model one on. We've cast ourselves
as the women, with a few other girls
who never dared to act out when alive.
Standing on the stage wall, we hold fast
and rejoice in our power.
                              Shame we had to die,
but, really, what have we lost? Desdemona had love
but it killed her, and it always was an uphill battle anyway,
being a free-thinking Venetian. Men think you're a whore
or, if you've enough languages, a courtesan.
Which she wasn't, but you, Iago,
couldn't bear any relationship that wasn't your own,
or even, apparently, the one that was.
You're not the wronged one, but you can't–or won't–see it.
I wish on you chilblains, eczema, the stoop of arthritis, scoliosis,

all the things that will make you look as you are,
a decrepit soul.
       At your death-bed,
only those hired to be with you will be.
One time I might have been there, washed
and anointed you, as a wife does, but that's a chore
and a duty too far. I don't miss you. Frankly, I've paid.

LADY MACBETH IN PALLIATIVE CARE

She didn't die after all, you see.
It was just the great quantity of blood,
the discarded flesh, and her desire to be
far away. Some servants are more loyal
than others. Not sure how she spent her life,
but she's a favourite here, with her inborn
manners and once, they say, a great wit.
I came late; I wouldn't know.

She doesn't say a great deal these days,
though she's still there, in her eyes, if you
understand what I mean. Some aren't.
She stays in her room, sits in the sun, with the
window wide open, spitting bluebottles to the wall
with the points of her perfect, stainless hooks.

CORDELIA IN PRISON

She is left a moment. Footsteps recede.
She can hear nothing familiar–even
the voice of her father a corridor, a world
away has a foreign lilt, a wind
from a place she has never seen.

Silence. Then metal approaches, swing
by clank, and the key turns. The locks,
she notes, are well-oiled here, do not
protest. There are terse-faced men who nod
but do not speak; who slide the rope out hushingly.

She had always known it ends in death.
She tries not to choke or sob, but go
quietly, as in stories. It is difficult.
The men turn away. Is she offending, again,
by saying nothing? She rattles. Grows wings.

THE WEIRD SISTERS ON THE MAKE

Before you think about going for immortality,
consider what might happen to your calling
over a thousand years' time. We three've stuck together
through thick and thin, and found
there's always demand for a quick prophecy.
But finding ingredients is a bitch.
Eye of newt and toe of frog?
Wool of bat and tongue of dog?
Unbelievable how precious people are
about animals these days. Take owlet's wing:
in the morning we found our place picketed
by people divided between grim purpose
(we liked that, and tried to recruit) and those
whose vocabulary didn't go beyond 'cute' and 'oh, but…'.
Still, we contrive and adapt.
Witches' mummy used to use flank fat
of a red-haired girl; now, on the quiet,
we raid liposuction clinics–pass a quick £50
now and again and swear not to examine DNA.
Lots of sharks on the shore if you look–
someone's lopped off their fins but we only need
mouth and teeth. Share and share alike.
Herbs are still okay, thank goodness.
No one seems to queue up for plants' rights.
And you wouldn't believe how hard
it is to find a good cauldron.
We mix it up in Syria, Korea, all those places.
Flying under our own steam, we don't need passports,
and we've learned to avoid radar.
Ancient institution, that's us. Tradition with invention.

To business: you work at a zoo? Could you put us wise
in the event of a baboon's demise?
No? We dare say you'd help if you could.
Look out for C-sections and walking woods.

MARGARET OF ANJOU

A world full of martial Henries, and I get the bookish one.
Ah, well, I have fire enough for the both of us,
and no fear of using it. Out of the wreckage around Orléans,
a dynasty. We will be strong. After all,
when the blood of war marries its like,
after a few generations conversation becomes impossible.
When I break my fast, he comes in... and *talks.*
It's strangely humbling, seeing his quiet eyes rapt
in contemplation of God or other smaller faiths,
like the one kept in the bedchamber. Our son takes after me.
When he wears the crown, his flame will illuminate the gold.
But Henry–my poor Henry–wears it as a crown of thorns.

The problem with saints is that too often they're martyrs.
York and the others plot in corners, and think
we don't notice. Henry may not, but I have more nous
than they credit me with, and will not lie by meekly.
They claim that he is mad, and mad he may be,
to those souls–and I use the term loosely–who cannot conceive
of a larger world.

                    I fear my husband
may lay down his cross and bow his weighted head.
I cannot but grieve for a gentle man
in ungentle times. But I gird myself. My son
is a skilled warrior, and I of a likeness
to Eleanor and other queens. Armed with his steel,
my wit, and our fire, we will fight to the death.

To the insurgents I will leave my curse: You thought
you were dealing with a girl, but you will suffer
at the weapons of a woman. Any crown you win
will be a paper one.

SHAKESPEARE'S JOAN

Only God above knows who I really am.
The rest pull and tug, and I fracture.
I'm La Pucelle to the French, holy champion.
They believe in me.
I did, too.

The English, though,
don't believe in either me or God.
It's inconvenient.
They see my country breeding
as an affront, a sign of
dark and desperate proclivities. Whatever that means.
Sorcery. That word's about the same,
and they use it often, claiming
my skills are hell-born, my visions delusion.
Apparently yesterday I fought someone
and straddled his defeated body, laughing.
(I was in council at the time,
in front of plenty of witnesses.)
The English soldiers, they slaver and leer as they talk.
They have never been innocent.

But stories change you. This morning I noticed
an ostler crossing himself after I spoke,
then making the sign. What can I say?
Forgiveness is part of His creed.
Maybe the ostler's Burgundian
or someone else played by foreigners.
The casting call was wide.

A lull now, a respite, intermission.

I've lost track of my entrances,
and fear my exits.

It's cold. Even in my gambeson
I shiver. My God, my God,
have you forsaken me?

The sky is silent.

PAULINA AS PYGMALION

Hermione, dear, come down and have a cup of tea.
Staring out the window won't make the time go by.
I should know. At least I can bring you titbits
of news from the court, all that evidence
they miss you. And we've had your sister's children here, too,
so you could watch them run around, or study.
My Latin wasn't as rusty as all that, was it?
I know, it was hard watching and not being able
to tell them who you were. But it was that
or prison–children never can keep a secret,
and your sentence stands. Your husband's a stubborn git.
Don't see he's worth the wait. No, no, I know,
there's just something about having a man in your bed,
and not just a bearskin. What is that something?
If we could answer, we'd solve the need for poetry
and plays.

       Oh, look here! Such lovely cakes. Snow in summer–
your favourite. I remember how you couldn't get enough
when we were girls. The times you'd eat yourself sick, then
                                   repent
when a pretty boy came along. You always were the pretty one,
and you know what? you still are, wrinkles and all.
Oh, I didn't mean to set you off. I know it's hard,
but we've been cosy, haven't we? It's not so bad, considering
the alternative. Hermione, dear, step off the plinth.
You'll have your happy ending soon.

HIS MOST FAMOUS WOMEN

Ophelia fell into an ill-defined love.
Hedged into iambs, hemmed by flowers,
she chose her sort of drowning over the other.

Lady M gave up her name to superstition,
then sacrificed everything else; found out
she wasn't even missed. Love, she thought,
shouldn't have this sort of small print, should
be written bold in bright blood-red.

Desdemona found love was defined by
jealous white men, had nothing to do with her.
Dying, she choked on its syllables.

Love speaks his soliloquies, ends in death.
Synonymise it with tragedy, marriage:
it never gives; is never hers–always revolves
around the Edenic apple of his I.

MARY ARDEN'S GARRETS

1. MARY ARDEN INN, WILMCOTE

At the mournful confluence of traffic, cows, and booze,
a stone's throw from where Shakespeare wasn't
even dreamed of, I lie in a room
my mother would approve of, thinking
how Mary wasn't as grand as the tea-towels said.

Domesday family, heiress,
yes, and then some, but not so black-and-white,
so picturesque as all that. How her marriage
was just as hasty as her son's in its way.
That shows chutzpah as well as lust, I'd say.

2. MARY IN HENLEY STREET

I miss
long vistas of treetops
outside my window,
my private ocean of leaves;

the slow-growing amber of the fields;
the seasonal percussion of thresher and scythe;

and secrets. Here shops are the thing–
no excitement
when the chapman comes back
with his case
and that bit of ribbon
mum mustn't know about,
and his story about the boy who left
who sends his love

though you know he doesn't,
not really.

Married to a man
who deals in skin,
the stench of tanning
is everywhere.
It makes truth taste different.
Although we've a good bed
and room enough.

What I miss most
is all the small myths
that defined me.
The breath I left behind.

3. HER FRIEND JONE MAKES THE TRIP TO
STRATFORD
The cushions on the guest bed are feather.
Not just the pillows. The cushions.
Dear God. No straw for Mary Arden.
Mary Shakespeare, they say now, and
Lord knows the wedding was quick enough
and the funeral meats hardly cold.
Joan born, poor mite, swift after.

But despite all that, her husband's
alderman, bailiff, what have you.
This fine house. A young son.
Feather beds. Lord, the beds.
Mary's landed on her feet, *I'd* say.

Note: Mary Arden came from a Warwickshire gentry family and married down to one of her father's tenant farmers, only a few days after the mandatory mourning period for her father. For many years the huge half-timbered house in Wilmcote was billed as 'Mary Arden's House' and used on souvenirs, but in 2000 it was found not to be old enough, and a more modest house nearby to have been in all probability Mary's.

WITH PAPER FOR FEET
SECTION FOUR

AFTER THE BATTLE

That's a tidy haul.
A dozen, maybe two,
to be taken off
for Christian burial.

Of course, a ring or two
don't go amiss
with the missus.
Not them big flashy ones–
those are missed, and anyways
the sort as wear them
usually get claimed. It's the poor sods
left behind I deal with, them
as believed fancy words
and died for 'em.
I pick 'em up,
put 'em on the cart.
Wife washes the bodies,
priest puts 'em in earth.

And why not us benefit
instead of the sodding magpies?
I'm a God-fearing man.
I don't take crosses.
You seen a summer battle
in the heat,
bodies swollen and fly-blown
almost before they fall,
you'd fear, too.
Though we got thrippence each
to dig a mass grave, that time,

cloths 'round our mouths
and not daring to eat for the smell.
Picking 'em up careful
so they don't burst.
God in heaven.

We cross ourselves every night,
say our prayers.
Shit and have shoes
same as you.

And wouldn't you rather
your man was cared for

than taken by scavengers?

I'm as good as it gets.

BLOODY CORNER [1]

It's not the press of bodies now.
Then, fifty men tried to cover their backs
as Alfred's men screamed, swords whirling
like the tarnished halos of a demented host.
We weren't the only ones to fall. Alfred suffered, too,
trod his own men beneath his feet
in the red mud. We tried to cover the king,
as harness and body protested.
Despite ourselves we looked to see
how much further we had to go; where
our ship lay fettered to the sands.
Fewer looked each time. Feet stumbled.
None of us knew mercy. We'd have done the same.
And then king against king. Fewer blows
than I'd have expected, all things considered.
No quarter. A great breath as Hubba fell,
knees buckling almost gently to earth; it was over.
Someone buried him. I'd like to say it was us,
but now, I can't remember. We all had wives and children,
and the tide was right.

Now, a dozen cars crowd a grumbling bus.
A caravan obscures our last words,
written in the colour of blood: Stop, stranger. Stop.

---

[1]In North Devon, there is a sharp bend in the Appledore road which is dubbed 'Bloody Corner.' On a wall at the corner, written in red on a dark stone plaque, is the following inscription: Stop stranger stop / Near this spot / Lies buried / King Hubba the Dane / Who was slain by / King Alfred the Great / In a Bloody Retreat / AD DCCCLXXXXII [sic].

MARGERY KEMPE

You, creature, laughed at life,
rollicked in bed, gave birth to
fourteen children and a genre.

You yearned for less, knew the blackness of
the months post-partum, men's lack
of care. Saved by your visions, you bought
your chastity, pacted with your husband
under the cross; changed your wide bed for
the uncertainty of foreign linens. Ecstatic pilgrim, your
tears were rivers that traversed continents.
You hit all the hotspots, bent knee to every saint,
insisted on your holiness. Creature, society doubted,
locked you up, but your heart strengthened in
solitude. Unfettered, unlettered, you bent men's
fingers to the page, knew the value of your words.

How we read them, dream
of a heart beyond bearing.

CUNNING FOLK

He
studied the stars to know folks' fate
collected piss when they took sick
sawed off their legs when he had to

I
gathered and dried plants
was gossip to the village
knew folks for miles around
and could name their great-grandfathers

He
had studied in the city
intoned Latin on the fly
could make a thief confess

I
learned at my mother's knee
bred squirrels for fur and dogs for hunting rats
(named 'em all) and spun a smooth thread

We
married. Together we
ushered in a generation of children
flushed others out of should-be maids
set bones and mended fences
After thirty years

He
died and was buried
a good Christian in the church
Three years later

I
was hanged

ANOTHER WITCH

If you're lucky, your friends come
and hang on your legs.
It's shorter then,
no half-words choking out of you
in mid-air.

More often, though, they're up there with you.
Friends, I mean. Neighbours, too.
Swinging in a wind
too heavy to feel.

I talked too much, asked
for what I could not have. They said,
Could not have. I said, Please.
I said some other things too, I suppose.
It's only natural.

In the dark, no bed,
bit of straw if you're lucky,
they ask you to talk some more,
and more. Had a kitten once, name of Jack,
poor thing, eyes still blue and no mum.
And me, no kids, I thought why not,
there's been no purring in the night for me now,
not for years. Fed him milk,
kept hanging on.
I was annoyed and proud both
day he was strong enough to draw blood.
Grew to be a regular terror.
Got run over by a cart one day;
cart-wheel came off, John broke his leg in the tumble.

Never saw him curse, change shape,
or ride through the night.
John, that is. The cat either.

Beg pardon, your worship,
but after three days without sleep
I can't tell you from the devil either.

Now it's just a matter
of revenge, or not.
There's Alice, she looked at me sideways
the other day, and Jennet,
she thinks it's funny being old.
A couple of others, too, known 'em for years.
We're friends, sometimes. Sometimes, well,
that's how it goes.
You choose who you want with you
that last time, for the last meeting,
for the thick, slow shading
into black.

NAN BULLEN

This time I would have made it:
I saw the look in his eye and backed down;
fired Jane; found the right herbs and produced
a proper heir. But I got tired of
eggshells, kowtowing, the sad eyes of
my devil-haired daughter. So I rewound
time again, had one last flaming row–
cut everything short at a thousand days.

LISTENING WOMAN

Once
she'd dreamt the spirits said,
If you ever see the sea, daughter,
you will never go home.
They used a different word for sea.
Her tongue had no name for it.
Her world was boundaried
by buffalo and sweetgrass smoke.

When the whitemen came
she began to walk
and to know the meaning of walls.

Time was measured
in her footsteps upon the earth.
The land echoed them back to her.

Gradually
the harsh calls of large white birds
replaced the songs in her heart.

Now
eyes closed
she stands on the shore
listening to the hiss and the slap and the pound
ever and over
ever and over
she dreams of sweetgrass smoke
and she trembles.

PHARAOH'S CONCUBINE

Of course he was divine.
He said so.

There are many types
of sacrifice. I was thirteen, just.
Pretty, straight nose, long neck,
a way of speaking. So they said.
Just shy, really.

All the gold, the pomp,
the myrrh-laced ceremonies, the solemn
and smoky intonations,
all the choreographed apparitions,
cowed me. As (I suppose) it was meant.

When at last he came to me,
I was shocked to see
two arms, two legs,
and not a falcon's head or even a jackal's,
but slightly uneven teeth,
dark, soft eyes,
and a pimple (expertly disguised).
I smiled.

The years passed
in rich, encoded rituals.
We both aged–both, it turned out,
kept our figures. When at last
his ka left him, I wept–
and was passed on.

And now, listening to the litanies
in the new temple
praising his ineffable divinity,
I sing the words
and do all that I ought.

But sometimes when I watch
Ra's solar barque passing,
I can't help wondering
if when they weigh my soul
he'll be clear-skinned and waiting,
and if he still snores.

DOROTHY KING RECALLS ROBERT HERRICK, VICAR OF DEAN PRIOR

Yes, I *am* ninety-eight. I can count,
you know. Anyways, the vicar was always on
about something. Life is short, he'd say. Seize
the day. Virgins. That sort of thing. Words got him
defrocked for a while. But then who needs
verse? I tell you what, the best thing about
him was that he taught his pig to quaff from
a tankard. We dared each other to drink the dregs.

WITH PAPER FOR FEET
SECTION FIVE

LILITH DREAMS AGAIN OF THE END OF TIME

I do not know that I dreamt, only that I sang
to a riddle of stars: *Who then? Who then?* and

no one voice answered; instead, inaudible,
a chorus of bass hosts, soprano needs.

I walked along deep waters, throwing names
into the rift, including yours. Including mine.

The rain that fell was no baptism, no shock of cold
birthing self, selves. I sang, walking, un-naming,

till I wore to footsteps; did no more than echo
against the dark-hearted and anonymous sky.

MARY MAGDALENE WALKS BY ANOTHER
CONSTRUCTION SITE

The words between my legs
are not as dangerous as
the words you spout about them.

The gazes hanging from my chest
are not as controlling as
the eyes you keep in your head.

When my legs move, sway
hip to hip, I am not a metronome
measuring your pulses of desire.

Nor am I just slot B for your tab A,
japanned in wolf whistles and *c'mere baby*s.
I long only for such flesh as my own,

so pray to that eternal male god
that he fold me into his nothingness
or grant me some small machinery of grace.

WHAT HISTORY DOES NOT RECORD

When the sword was raised, the real mother screamed.
Solomon gave her her baby back.
Court dismissed. Noticing the pout
on the face of the impostor, Solomon gestured.
Come, he said, *I'll give you a baby.*
So this is wisdom, she thought, as incense
poured over the bed. (The servants,
going about their business,
were too practised to notice the grunts.)

DINAH

If they could see
the darkened sky,
the proud smile; feel
the roughened, selfish hands–
If they could hear
the laughter,
the mocking words,
the grunts like pigs...
I would shake them from their semantics,
would cry out as I cry in dreams.
But they do not listen,
these humanists, these exegetes
who rape me again with their words.

So I am silent.
It is, after all, my brothers' story.

JUDITH AND HOLOFERNES

A king is like a god,
Holofernes says.
Our quarrel is with Nebuchadnezzar,
not with him.
He is, however, the one who's here
with a sword and an army.

It's not easy for me
to go into his tent
and suffer his touch.
I mean it is easy–
it works like a charm.
But.

'Widow' is a magic word.
We're gagging for it, honest.
Apparently all men know this.

Does he know
my husband gave me this dress
and that it still smells of him?
That as we couple
I imagine a hundred other faces
praying to the rightful God?

When I leave I give his servant
a filthy wink. He turns his head.
I escape, bag dripping.

Later, I ride into Bethulia.
The head is heavy.
I hold it high.

PILLAR

Lot's wife paused
in the flight from Gomorrah;
shifted her pack. Heard–
perhaps–the sounds of destruction.
Thought–perhaps–of what
her daughters had carefully
not told her. Looked back.

They left her there, solid tears
under a sky empty of everything
except a lone seraph, singing.

LOT'S WIFE CONSIDERS REINCARNATION

I.

if i came back as a snail
i would learn many things

how dampness is life-giving
how you are your home's best ornament

that birds' beaks are sharp
and feet are in the main crushingly heavy

i would learn many things
but i still wouldn't like salt

II.

if i came back as a cockroach
i would relearn my instinct to hide
until night brought bravery

the skitter-patter of my six feet
would find the secret cracks
where bare subsistence dwelt

i would survive by fragments
entire

III.

if I came back as a mosquito
i would comprehend my dependence on others

IV.

if i came back as a locust
i would finally understand
my eternal hunger for you

V.

if i came back as a dung beetle
i wouldn't learn much
except life is shit and always has been

and who doesn't get that
the first time around

MORTIFICATIONS OF THE FLESH
after Colm Tóibín

Every mother has a crown of thorns.
Here is mine: my things of which I am ashamed.

  I could not teach him to admire his father.

  I could not keep him from arguing with his elders.

  As he got older, he adopted a fake posh accent.

  I did not like his friends, or understand them.

  I could not bear to hear them laughing after midnight.

  I could never make him wear his hair neatly.

There are a few more.
Like how I feared for my own life.
Like how I turned my face from him.
Even more, like when seeing his suffering
the soldiers paused, how I snapped.
  'If you're going to do it, do it,' I said.
  'For the love of God. Here, you dropped a nail.'

SINGING HOSANNA

If you go to the holy hill
and lie down with your picture of Jesus
he will put himself inside you
and make you real.

Lie in the copse
where no one can hear your ecstasies.
Your breath will come short
and shorter
till the moment you gasp
hosanna–oh–hosanna–
and collapse on the moss,
knowing you have passed
beyond the edge
of any beginning
and this is the real thing:
under your veil is a woman,
not a girl.

And when singing at mass
you catch breath
remembering the time you had none
the other sisters will nod
and you will decorate the cross together
and know what votives are for:

calling come back, come back,
all is forgiven.

SECRETARY OF GOD
Our Lord has often revealed his secrets to the world
through women. – Christine de Pisan

These are not my words.
I drank God straight from the well.

I move through hours.
Predictions drip and pool.

When they burn the fields,
I taste ash. Tell me

this isn't beautiful. I sink
downwards, a red moon

paling and losing its breath,
words coming from nowhere.

Write it like revelation:
this white, white light.

ABOUT THE AUTHOR

Jennifer A. McGowan lives in Oxford. Despite being certified as disabled with Ehlers-Danlos syndrome at age 16, she became a semi-professional mime and performed in five countries till the disability became too much. More recently she has worked as researcher, editor, and writer for a UK company in "devil's advocacy". She has taught both under- and postgraduates at several universities, in subjects as varied as English, history, and heritage studies. Her poems have appeared in many literary journals on both sides of the Atlantic, including *The Connecticut Review, Gargoyle, Storm Cellar, Envoi, Acumen,* and *Agenda* (which also featured her mediaeval calligraphy and illumination); her first chapbook, *Life in Captivity* and *Sounding* are available from Finishing Line Press. Her work has also been anthologised in *Birchsong* (Blue Line Press, 2012), *A Moment of Change* (Aqueduct Press, 2012), and *The Other Side of Sleep* (Arachne Press, 2015). Songs she has written have been recorded on several labels.
http://www.jenniferamcgowan.com/

ACKNOWLEDGMENTS

These poems or versions of them first appeared in the following publications, and some of them have won commendations or prizes:

1000 Monkeys anthology: *Lot's Wife Considers Reincarnation*
Acumen: *Pythoness; Helen: Menelaus, etc.*
Agenda (online supplement): *Shakespeare's Joan*
British Science Fiction Association's journal: *Something About Love*
The Dark Horse: *Briar Roses*
Enchanted Conversation: *Song of Krampus; The Talking Skull; Love Like Salt*
Arachne Press' The Other Side of Sleep and Envoi: *Troy Seven Voices*
Hermes Poetry Journal: *Icarus*
Ink, Sweat & Tears: *Secretary of God*
The Interpreter's House: *What History Does Not Record*
Life in Captivity (Finishing Line Press, 2011): *Pharaoh's Concubine, Phantom Pains, Tempus Fugue, The Maiden Without Hands, Another Witch*
The North: *Bloody Corner*
Manchester Cathedral Competition Booklet: *Margery Kempe*
Orbis: *Curandero; Mr Fox*
Prole: *Mortifications of the Flesh; Mary Magdalen Walks by Another Construction Site; Dorothy King Recalls Robert Herrick, Vicar of Dean Prior; A Sort of Love Story; Singing Hosanna*
Rustic Rub: *Mara Speaks*
The Rialto: *White Woman Walks Across China with Paper for Feet*
The Screech Owl: *Judith and Holofernes*
Star*Line: *The Witch-Box*
Weyfarers: *In Granny's House*
YorkMix: *Cordelia in Prison*

ABOUT ARACHNE PRESS
www.arachnepress.com

Arachne Press is a micro publisher of (award-winning!) short story and poetry anthologies and collections, novels including a Carnegie Medal nominated young adult novel, and a photographic portrait collection. We are very grateful to Arts Council England for financial support for this book and three others, a tour round the UK and our live events.

We are expanding our range all the time, but the short form is our first love.

The Solstice Shorts Festival

(http://arachnepress.com/solstice-shorts)

Now in its third year, Solstice Shorts is all about time: held on the shortest day of the year on the Prime meridian, stories, poetry and song celebrate the turning of the moon, the changing of the seasons, the motions of the spheres, and clockwork!

The Story Sessions

(http://arachnepress.com/the-story-sessions)

We showcase our work and that of others at our own bi-monthly live literature event, in south London, which we run like a folk club, with headliners and opportunities for the audience to join in.We are always on the lookout for other places to show off, so if you run a bookshop, a literature festival or any other kind of literature venue, get in touch; we'd love to talk to you.

Follow us on Twitter: @ArachnePress @SolShorts
Like us on Facebook: ArachnePress, SolsticeShorts2014, TheStorySessions

BOOKS FROM ARACHNE PRESS

POETRY OUT NOW:

Foraging by Joy Howard ISBN: 978-1-909208-39-1

POETRY BACK LIST:

The Other Side of Sleep: Narrative Poems
ISBN: 978-1-909208-18-6

Long, narrative poems by contemporary voices, including
Inua Elams, Brian Johnstone, and Kate Foley, whose title
poem for the anthology was the winner of the 2014 *Second
Light* Long Poem competition.

The Don't Touch Garden by Kate Foley
ISBN: 978-1-909208-19-3

A complex autobiographical collection of poems of adoption
and identity, from award-winning poet Kate Foley.

SHORT STORIES COMING APRIL 2017:
Happy Ending NOT Guaranteed by Liam Hogan
ISBN: 978-1-909208-36-0
Deliciously twisted fantasy stories.